TIME TO COMPARE

Which IS LONGER?

T0009944

first concepts

BY JAGGER YOUSSEF

Gareth Stevens
PUBLISHING

We can compare!
The orange pencil
is longer.

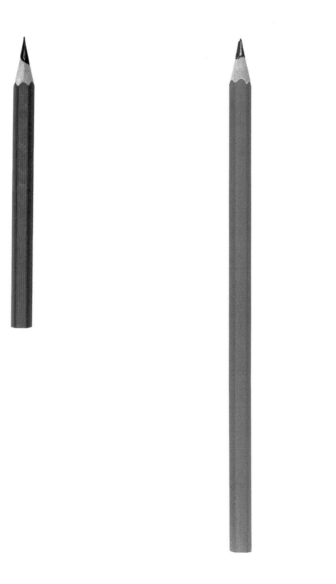

3

The black truck
is longer.

The pink ruler
is longer.

7

The yellow balloon is longer.

9

The white box
is longer.

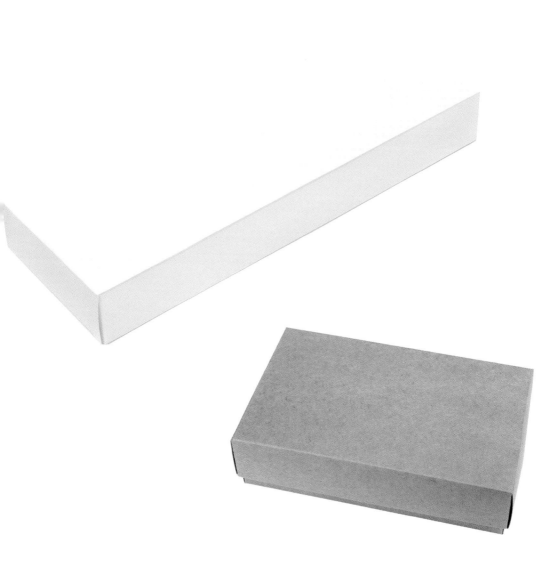

The purple crayon is longer.

13

The red candy
is longer.

15

The brown shoes are longer.

17

The black table
is longer.

19

The green snake
is longer.

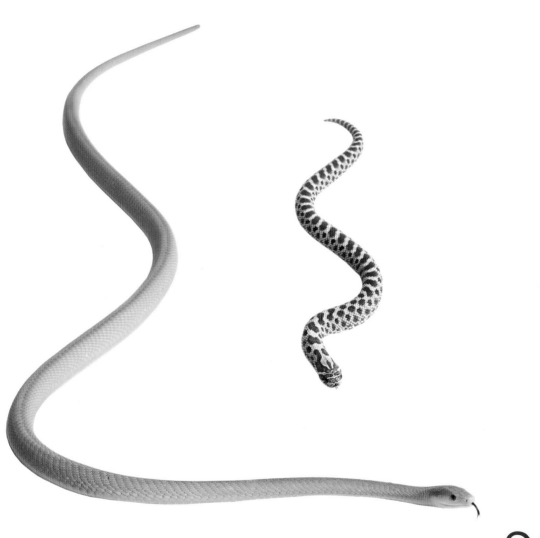

21

Point to the
longer train.

23

Please visit our website, www.garethstevens.com. For a free color catalog of all our high-quality books, call toll free 1-800-542-2595 or fax 1-877-542-2596.

Library of Congress Cataloging-in-Publication Data
Names: Youssef, Jagger, author.
Title: Which is longer? / Jagger Youssef.
Description: New York : Gareth Stevens Publishing, [2021] | Series: Time to compare | Includes index.
Identifiers: LCCN 2019043392 | ISBN 9781538255162 (library binding) | ISBN
    9781538255148 (paperback) | ISBN 9781538255155 (6 pack)| ISBN
    9781538255179 (ebook)
Subjects: LCSH: Length measurement–Juvenile literature. | Size
    judgment–Juvenile literature. | Comparison (Psychology) in
    children–Juvenile literature.
Classification: LCC QC102 .Y68 2021 | DDC 530.8–dc23
LC record available at https://lccn.loc.gov/2019043392

First Edition

Published in 2021 by
Gareth Stevens Publishing
111 East 14th Street, Suite 349
New York, NY 10003

Copyright © 2021 Gareth Stevens Publishing

Translator: Cecilia González Godino
Editor, Spanish: Natzi Vilchis
Designer: Sarah Liddell
Editor: Therese Shea

Photo credits: Cover, p. 1 (main) Direk Yiamsaensuk/Shutterstock.com; cover, p. 1 (background) oksanka007/
Shutterstock.com; p. 3 Satori Studio/Shutterstock.com; p. 5 (black truck) Dario Lo Presti/Shutterstock.com; p. 5 (yellow
truck) Adisa/Shutterstock.com; p. 7 (green ruler) photastic/Shutterstock.com; p. 7 (pink ruler) OlekStock/Shutterstock.com;
p. 9 (yellow balloon) Gyvafoto/Shutterstock.com; p. 9 (red balloon) pukach/Shutterstock.com; p. 11 (white box) Roman
Samokhin/Shutterstock.com; p. 11 (brown box) Sichon/Shutterstock.com; p. 13 Natee Photo/Shutterstock.com; p. 15
(red candy) BW Folsom/Shutterstock.com; p. 15 (black candy) Hong Vo/Shutterstock.com; p. 17 (red shoes) Miss Ty/
Shutterstock.com; p. 17 (brown shoes) Anna Klepatckaya/Shutterstock.com; p. 19 (black table) kibri_ho/Shutterstock.com;
p. 19 (brown table) donatas1205/Shutterstock.com; p. 21 (green snake) Eric Isselee/Shutterstock.com; p. 21 (orange
snake) fivespots/Shutterstock.com; p. 23 (top) Evgeny Karandaev/Shutterstock.com; p. 23 (bottom) taviphoto/
Shutterstock.com.

CPSIA compliance information: Batch #CS20GS: For further information contact Gareth Stevens, New York, New York at 1-800-542-2595.